It Started by Noticing

By

Glenn McLaughlin

Published in the US by Absurdly Normal Books.

First Edition, 2025

ISBN: 978-0-9779728-4-5

Cover design and interior layout by Krista Somers.
Cover painting, "Untitled Watercolor, 1975", by Glenn R. McLaughlin
Back cover photo by Charles Pulliam

Copies available at www.lulu.com or from the author.

For A.V. Christie and Daniel Hoffman
who first believed

Table of Contents

Introduction: A Breath

there was that condescending comment
about poetry being like a diary, too voyeuristic

there are some, the ones we have all written
but it is the ones that go beyond the personal

diary pages all the way to normal things

are the ones that stop your heart
and breathe for you for a moment:

after the rain stops and the filtering
water through maple leaves continues

seed the squirrels have not stolen
has fallen from the feeder during the storm

but not washed away because of the maple
(hands catch things, soften them)

cardinals, male and female, manage
look dry even flying

through the storm and splashed puddles
eat the seed, sing and light the patio

this is nothing for a journal
just for your heart and a breath

62998

a pauper's grave

they speak when the wind
gives them voice again
their mouths always open
waiting for air

this one walked and sang
once, even moaned
I am certain moaned
cried in private nights

thinking no one heard
deep in the forest
surrounded and alone
probably no one did

and in falling there was
a sound as air moves away
there is always a sound
always touch on the way

down, sliding past another
into the ground where pine knots
from new growth are exposed
worthless except for this

the chorus greater by one
and more souls added each day
speaking, singing, crying
touching the wind

A Comparison

my rhododendron freezes quickly and curls her broad leaves
un-sharpened pencils or cigars to some
those that know think the curls fill with small ice
crystals that thaw only slowly, preserving the leaf

...

you freeze quickly, she says, when you realize
then curl inside yourself to hide
so no one will know, you cover yourself
in ice that thaws only slowly, to safely preserve

...

each branch end is an unlit ornament
tipped with a tight green bulb
anticipating June
blazing violet

for Andrea - hope that even at eighty
there will come a day when she blooms
as her true self

A Memoir: Upon Viewing Michelangelo's "Pieta"

don't you want them
words drawn from air
as those images from marble

don't you
want:

the love in eyes without irises
the touch of that marble flesh
the layer of fat under her feminine skin
the sinew of his muscle, even dead

don't you want that in your words
that moment of transformation
that has nothing to do with this world
      or time

but has everything to do with stone
      and foundation

New York City World's Fair, 1964

A Prayer Drawn from Holy War

help me understand why
when You stepped aside
emptied a space within You
for Your creation of us
the connections You left
     the shimmering in air
     the unexplained and mysterious
seem to be waves of understanding, substance
     that escape our grasp

why
when standing on Your circle
we each see a different face
and then in turning
     still connected by Your locus
we look past You
and beyond the opposite
ignoring ties and equal distances

help me understand why, how
we, all here engaged, say we have listened
to Your voice, spoken at once to each
believing each is the first and only to clearly hear

could the sound have been just an echo for all:
truth broken by walls
changed by stepping away from You

A preemptive apology, a year later

I want to apologize in advance of advancing
past the time when I'll forget to remember
who I am or who you are, or we are, every day.
That used to be a joke but is now my fear
having found the wish. I apologize
for wanting more memories to forget,
each moment a jewel to misplace.
And I hope I remember – now, and then –
that it is so easy to forget what it was,
and what it could have been, without you.

For Sue

A Thought in the Wake

December 5th, 11:30 PM

on the night when snow was first predicted to fall
it was brilliantly dark at first then lightened as clouds
      the first suggestion of clouds
drew up from the south in a motion that was nearly
snow blown off of a ridge or a drift in mid-winter
not enough to block all of your sight but enough
to hide all but the planets and brightest stars
      which still shone but now with halos
closer, trees became more visible and the chill
      began to cut through coats

and while that could have been the poem, I thought
it really was that I thought I could hear the wind approach
carrying the storm after the geese flew out of earshot
leaving just a hint of their wake
through the slowly streaming clouds

and while that could have been the poem, I thought
it really was that I had a moment, and the luxury
      for the thought
of geese and their gentle wake through clouds

In Eastern states, many barns constructed in the 18th and early 19th centuries were built with timber harvested from the land on which they were erected.

During the Civil War, the doors from many barns near battlefields were taken and used as operating tables to treat wounded soldiers of both sides. Some doors were returned to their barns.

In the late 20th and early 21st centuries, as urban expansion and a changing economy decimated many old family farms, the barns were dismantled and the lumber machined to make high-end flooring materials for very expensive new homes. While no families appear to be without some sort of hardship, a fair generalization is the families that now walk on the floors made from these old barns have issues substantially removed from those of Civil War era soldiers fighting and dying for their visions of liberty and country.

A Short History of a Barn and His Door

...

before 1854
before the Amish
everyone just helped

a barn was the land re-formed
hung tobacco, housed hay
held stories of families
          the good and the bad days

...

there were many horses
and soldiers, wagons and iron cannon
there were cries and running to hide

soldiers came for his door
and the barn watched open-mouthed, amazed

the door did not know *doctor*
was different from *carpenter*
both cut when men fell

sounds fell on his grain like rain
stormed trembling then silent

...

some doors came home, some did not
and like many of the men who came home
stood silent

their stories buried in their grain
where blood had run beneath buckets of water

...

some years there was whitewash
some a local red paint
never years in a row

but never far below the surface
were the lives whose blood had run there

...

war, he never saw again
but heard
the women crying
the men crying
he could not speak his stories
just felt their pain in his grain

...

tobacco and hay
cows and horses
maybe a bin of oats or corn
the knowledge of barns
what do they know of economy or money
and the changing of things

...

how many young
had loved within him
for the first time

how many old
for the last

...

children leave
they don't return

parents and families die
so too, farms

and barns

...

he was among the first
grew from this earth
and was always a part

now he is among the last
to leave

...

underfoot a door remembers
severed arms and legs
feet and hands left pointing
life spilled after cries of freedom

underfoot a door thinks
he had seen it all
then thinks again

Ablate

he always fascinated me   the word

I felt the need to change   him

from the first introduction
the use beyond common definition   violent

stretching himself or someone directing
further than we, or he, knew

                                                 this time

polyethylene taken to plasma   to light

                                                 ablation

second wave of convergence
striking the match, a glimpse of

                                                 the power of God
                                                 of something we cannot

ablate from our consciousness

a child misjudged, placed wrongly
a circumstance of acquaintance

within himself: actions
rapid   precise   focused

         he viewed himself more innocently –
the movement of dew from a daffodil at sunrise
a prism transformed to the fullness of air
a trumpet of sunburst less weighted
a daily coating ... ablated

And there is water, Part 5: Body and Blood

pull the flesh from bone
peel a layer away
and press it to your tongue

roll it in your mouth
keep it
while you stare
ahead or down

or close your eyes to feel it blossom
and the bouquet bloom through your sinus
let it rush out your eyes and to your brain
let your stomach
         that empty pit
demand

then let the blood and the body touch
again, in your mouth

let them wash your throat clean
and the warmth that was on your tongue
become a cool wave that spreads
through your chest as water flowing in spring

savor the bread and the juice
savor the life and the touch
let them melt into you
naturally as food: savor
the soul and the new

After Nick Died

My wife had known Nick for most of the time since his grandparents had given him up to the state. They had gotten him from his parents after they had given up on him, though many said they hadn't really tried. And many said it was the last fire Nick had set, the one that had burned down the bleachers at the football stadium that had finally broken his grandparents. My wife met him after all that, when nearly everyone spoke poorly of him, though she never did. And she had known him since that one insightful and courageous caseworker had discovered that Nick really just wanted to be more like a girl and had let him grow his nails and hair and began to adjust his wardrobe even though all of that was against the rules, but everyone knew it was harmless and that the understanding, the kindness, had made all the difference.

One day in mid-June I stood in his room for the first time. The space was barely longer and wider than his single bed, where he spent his days now, but the room did have two windows. I was told it had come to this: whispers on the edge of not knowing when the line would be crossed to another life. Whispers because that was all he could manage and that was all the louder anyone else wanted to talk about what was going to happen next, happen soon, and they were sad and scared along with him.

There were "Titanics" everywhere – models, movie posters, sketches he had drawn of the actors, books about the ship and what had happened. The sketches were drawn in his own hand, as were the interspersed drawings from therapy, which were more childish, or, you might say, primitive. Standing apart from it all was a clay head, a bust but somewhat less, of him, made by him, scared and scaring, much as his life had been, I thought. I turned from it to him just as he asked my wife, "Can I borrow twenty so I can go shopping?" He promised to pay it back as soon as he could. She turned to me and asked for my wallet. She knew we would never see him again.

It must have happened early that mid-week morning in July while we were at The Cape, that morning after the night so thick I'd imagined I could see raindrops forming in mid-air to fall and run along the veins of leaves. But even that quiet and heavy evening air was transient, so by morning virtually all motion had gone away, leaving just quarter inch surf in the pond, silent vibrations from a setting moon, crashing in whispers against the reeds.

That must have been him leaving.

It was so still.

August

pluck a jaundiced moon
flip it from your forefinger with your thumb
watch it twist through the night

leap standing as a shadow into the branches of an oak
surround the katydids, hold them from sight
as they surround you with sound

lie with dogs in grass at midnight
watch currents drift past a streetlamp
imagine fish lazing and a hint touching rushes

can • ti • le • ver [kan-tl-ee-ver] *noun*: 1. any rigid structural member projecting from a vertical support, esp. one in which the projection is great in relation to depth, so that the upper part is in tension and the lower part in compression

ex.: *Fallingwater* designed by Frank Lloyd Wright; a parent bending at 90° at the waist to kiss a child (the latter example being a non-traditional association of the noun).

Cantilever

Some are thrusts
just to thrust

I saw one: a beautiful prosthetic
for something a stone hillside never had

Some are words thrown on air
their soul steeling them straight

I saw one: bending at her waist
straight to a whisper

Some, then, are grace:
an extension, a touching, of strength

Beech Street, Pottstown, Pa.

A suite of four poems

i. At Beech and Rosedale

One night, sitting at the gateway
the four-way stop at Rosedale
a leaf fell
landed on its edge and bounced
landed on its edge again, and waited
supported by the light of my headlights
till a small cloud from the tree above
fell just off-center and the leaf toppled
face up or face down, I could not tell.
As with all these lives nearby
I could not tell.

ii. Edgewood Elementary

There was a windstorm that took fall's leaves early
but not the children's recess as they tried to fly
with jackets unzipped, spread on arms
rushing west into her as fast as they could.

iii. Past The Hill School

Old presses hard against new, folding
on each other like layers of earth.
The Hill looks down on corners
where steel mills are long closed

where now the steel is already forged
barreled and rifled, and the ore-brown
smoke of the long cold ovens is a memory
from before the corner boys were born

18

though it seems to color the whites
of their eyes as they stand at midnight
on the corners between the churches'
stained glass windows bright to the street.

Lit by glowing exit signs inside,
the brownstones yield to brick
then to shingles and rotting siding
in places where time swirls directionless.

There is no understanding here
of Darfur, Afghanistan, or Gaza
when at Franklin, Evans or Charlotte
there is a country I do not know.

iv. One night, standing just off Beech

That day I lost my job, I watched the news
from Afghanistan and Iraq, then outside
heard the shooting just off Beech.

I did not stop breathing
nor was I unable to walk
I did not become deaf or blind
I noticed the sun set nearly at the same time
            as it did yesterday although it was a bit colder
I was not yet wiser for the experience
for it was too soon to hope my arms could embrace more
understand more of the world.

Here, there are summer grasses grown tall
            turned yellow, ochre
there, halfway around the world,
            there are summer grasses grown tall,
            turned yellow, ochre.
Both flow in a breeze, bend in the wind
            break under ice.

Here, there is a clear moon, there
        maybe a few clouds skipping across
        ones that may have been here first
Here, there were cicadas, locusts and crickets not long ago
there, I don't know having never spent a night.

Here, snow will soon cover a rock gently
        in a rush of silence
there, snow will cover a rock gently
        and silence, if there is a moment
        will rush in also, a surprise, I suspect.

There, there may be another color with the snow
        there probably is another color with the snow
        a primary color ...

Red in a black night is black, hiding as earth
        not covered by snow.

            It is the echo of a heartbeat.

Here, in my yard, there is only earth.
I can touch it all, feel the freeze of winter
        the thaw of a warm day.
I can touch silence for it has rushed and settled here
but I can also hear a shot that cracks through the air
and nearby see that it is not just earth that scars the snow.

I did not stop breathing that day
nor was I unable to walk
I did not become deaf or blind
I noticed the sun set at nearly the same time
        as it had the day before, although it was a bit colder
I was not yet wiser for this experience
for it was too soon to hope my arms could embrace more
understand more of the world.

Christina

Christina was born with cerebral palsy. I met her when she was twelve. She had long since run out of her own fingers and toes, and those of her relatives as well, to record the number of operations she'd had in the attempts to unfold her. All they had done was to keep her from folding in upon herself and disappearing. She did, however, fit perfectly into the soft plastic of a child's swing.

(Swinging as if another child running and playing
hair tossed wind full in her face as trees move
in and out of her stationary sight)

His name is in hers, is He also I wondered
while studying the cross, newly white with three spikes
and a lily to remind us of promise, to remind us He is here

Though I doubted when she cried, folded as if swinging
Mommy make it stop, make the pain go away

Studying the cross, newly white, I heard another cry
I'd been taught the answer to His, but I still asked about *her why*

(Swinging as if another child running and playing
hair tossed wind full in her face as trees move
in and out of her stationary sight)

She said she loved the trees in her window
and to swing with them in the breeze, a wish
for days without crying and more days like these

I've listened for His voice through her laughter and tears
and thinking I've heard Him wondered if He is here again, near

Folded together, swinging, as if a new child running and playing
hair tossed wind full in *their* face as trees move in and out of *their* sight

Bob*

Upon the birth of Lucy, my second granddaughter

He got sleepy while driving and pulled in under a tree
at the side of the road

You should know I stole that line from another poet,
a translated Nobel Laureate and that I changed the first word
because then it was what my father told me about Bob
back when Bob sold stationery and hated it
how he used to disappear because he thought it was all pointless
except for the money but then, what was the point of that, too?

Then there was that day he found himself in the middle place
in those moments between nap and waking
that place where you dream of what could be
of what isn't real
and he heard God speak.

Though not really speak
not like crazy people do
not with page after page of specifics and names
places and tasks
horror.

No, it wasn't like that at all
it wasn't like anything else – ever
it just was
something:
warm, loving, absolute
and he knew.

He never sold office supplies again
he never boasted about it
he just told my dad one day
something in conversation
maybe meant for me, maybe not.

22

And though I never heard anything so clearly
(or maybe I just wasn't listening enough)
I'm glad he did.

As were those who attributed the miracles to him.

But I
I attributed presence and assurance
while he gave water
poured water over my daughter
transforming it from cool and metaphor
to holding her
blessed.

And though I hear he often sleeps again
wakes, lost from what had been him
I think of him now
as my daughter holds her daughter
new, days old.

I think of him transforming water
a blessing, a gift, grace
that led to this.

*Bob Hoag is a former pastor of the First Presbyterian Church of Clarks Summit, PA

23

Clear in New Hampshire

Bright, the full moon drew up the lake into a fog
so thick the next morning it rained from the pines as dew
and with each drop less water floated, and maples began
to step from hiding in their gold, red, and orange coats
apparitions casting no reflections in the mirror where a raft
more than floated, moved through space as mist devils unwound
themselves disappearing, the lake settling back into itself
a drop, a wisp, at a time.

at Lake Winnipesaukee

Coffee without mania

There was a man in our town who walked for miles, gesticulating wildly, talking to no one we saw. One day, I saw him sitting, motionless, at a coffee shop table, staring into his cup of coffee with a pill bottle in his hand. My wife said she knew what he was thinking, debating – keeping the mania alive, the colors and the thrill, by weathering the darkness of depression versus taking the pill to "level" his world and steal the colors from him

Now is like this coffee muddied
with everything added, still brown
it holds neither the bite of cold
nor the sting of heat
no green soft spring or gold crisp fall
no thunder, lightning or even the thrill
of looking directly into the sun

Now is like this coffee muddied
I can add this pill again
or not

Contemplating a Life

Upon the death of Millvina Dean
last known survivor of the Titanic

I placed a lump of brown sugar
loose on my tongue
melting sweet sand, grainy velvet

I stood by roses, unexpectedly perfect
somehow thick and delicate at once
black within red making a fabric

luscious against the skin
soft against the tongue
I tried to tie them together

but one melted and the other died:
memory and loss
I imagined

Drops of ocean

One must have a mind of winter – Wallace Stevens from "The Snow Man"

they wanted to be ice and magnificent in their attempt
leaping into the air trusting in distance and independence
to fulfill their dream

they failed, they blamed it on their impurity, that portion so unlike
but a part of them, always a part of them
from their awakening

they all had it, split in two within them: metal bursting to flame,
if left alone, the other part a part of mustard, part of gas and
death, not seed

they dreamed of myriad combinations in crystal groups by joining
hands and feet, locking arms and legs in dazzling arrays
displays of strength and art

they thought of this spectacle as they flew before they were drawn
back again, before they tried again, and failed again
undaunted

they never knew they had already achieved the beauty
of their passion in the futility of their effort and its inspiration
so singular were they of mind

all they knew was trying over and over and over again, never giving up

I felt them, some of them, those that flew longer, touched,
then slipped away my hand wiping the salt and they, more pure,
dripped from my chin glistening

together in sunlight they refracted
together in moonlight they reflected
someday, soon, quietly ablated

they will become rain and snow

Dry

without music
this is dry, as Morrison would say

it has not a Lakewood gift to assure
success and wealth with its writing

it finds no home for sixty billion drops
lost in a bucket somewhere
so, they will stay with whomever has them

it is just dry

without a window opened to listen to rain
because even the rain has stopped

gone dry leaving just trees
their leaves releasing what they had held

and that sound is drier
a different gun or drum tumbling afar

lingering then disappearing
drifting under katydid and crickets

and still this page is dry

without a dog snoring or a woman to hold
they have both gone to bed

it has no coffee
barely enough light

no clock to tick or hum
no cars to splash puddles in the night

it has cats, though only sleeping ones
nearly as quiet as tomorrow's morning glories ready to bloom

So, this is just dry
even with rain, flowers, crickets and pets
and love not far away

Parched
as Morrison would say
unless the music is in you

*Jim Morrison, lead singer of The Doors,
often recited his lyrics "dry", to test if they
were as good without music*

Entropy and Enthalpy

I.

To prove his point, that complexity could not arise from simplicity or chaos, a man took apart his own jet airplane, set the parts in neat piles, and waited. And waited knowing full well the parts would just sit there in piles. He ignored what was around him, did not understand that the rule said that what was around him was part of this, too, that his piles were meaningless. And then he railed at *The Wind*, at *The Wind* of all things, saying only he, the man, had heard, only he knew. Only he didn't know.

Eventually, he left but not certain of which direction to go he typed the destination into his GPS and then followed, without question, the voice he had chosen. Certain now of his path, his time, and certain of time, he told me how much time there had been, he told *The Wind* how much time there had been, and strode away confident, certain.

And the four clocks, all with different time, faster and slower at once, kept him from falling off a cliff, just as they would anyone, and *The Wind* blew, just as it always had, waiting for someone to listen.

II.

I watched the young oak grow.
I watched the old pine die.

I watched mist rise from a lake at sunrise.
I watched dew fall and disappear.

I measured those changes
And I knew that was all I could do.

I looked up and out into a bounded and boundless expanding sky
And I knew I could not know all.

Eye-light

it was altocumulus in an arc
being pushed by wind from the west

it could have been a white quilt
bunched, left on a bed after a nap

it was sun at 6PM on an August evening
above a comma of clouds framed by clear sky

it could have been the light they speak of
shining through a tear in the fabric between now and next

it was just sunlight through cloud breaks
reflections, half columns of lit moisture, dust and pollen

it could have been the eye-light of children looking up
light and love: a coherent radiance as spotlights
slowly rising to touch you and God

First, I listened to the war

March 22, 2003

that evening I noticed
the drought had ended

there was a lake where there almost hadn't been
and the moon rose over it

the fog had gone earlier
as quickly as it had arrived

I stopped and heard crickets
and wondered how many bulbs were piercing

or leaf buds blooming, or neighbors
and friends I had seen that day

a fortunate spring

Fluid Dynamics

the turbulence is evident in the clouds
in the high southern wind fighting against the geese

in the tugging of gravity miles above and the falling
against the draw of space's emptiness wanting to be filled

smoke would trace the paths and trails
the designs of dance and march

but at the boundary here on the surface: laminar
tonight: independence from pressure and velocity

the trees breathe and their breaths are suspended
tied to the skin more viscous

you cannot hear them due to the stopping of sound
due to the independence from time

For the Ayn Rand Institute on Thanksgiving

from within the safety of walls
she wrote and asked

But how do you know the wind blows
if there are no leaves on the trees

for her candles did not flicker
nor did her fire waver in the hearth
her drapes hung heavy and straight
while the only sound she heard
the only movement she saw
was heat rising

How do you know?
that question again
asked in turning away from the window

just then, a response arrived, whispered
as if a breeze had gone before being noticed

Stand here, with us, outside
with the leaves gone from trees and ground
naked, nothing to clutch for warmth

Stand with whom, she offered matter-of-factly
turning to the warm fire once more
not noticing at all who had spoken

In response to Ms. Debi Ghati
"An Ayn Rand Thanksgiving: You've Earned It!"
The Philadelphia Inquirer, November 22, 2007

Fractal of Morning

*Fractal analysis is a method that uses statistical models and non-traditional
mathematics to examine characteristics of data, patterns, and processes.*

the thought came before the sun rose
but after the approach had begun,
the analysis of the fractal of morning:

do the colors affect the measure
does it change with the turn of pastel
to the piercing crossing the edge

or the building of blue from somewhere
on the fringes of sight by seconds, then minutes
and what of trees and do leaves matter

or do the myriad of intersections in winter
replace them with another solution
do the shadows matter, their color

close-black to steel-blue flowing across
snow melting apace with the motion
and does it matter to look straight

or hang out of the window, look left, right
up, down, and do the snowdrops matter or add
even if it is only at the fifth decimal?

in an instant, I suppose not, but the woodpecker
working in the old dying maple
the woodpecker does

From Mary Jo, for us

The day after Flossie Schumacher's 93rd birthday was a Sunday which was important because it meant Mary Jo, barely sixty, was there, too, while we sang "Happy Birthday" it did not matter whether or not I could see Flossie because I knew we were all thinking, though maybe from a slightly different angle, about that number, about its difference from twenty or fifty or even eighty-eight and that stayed with me as we moved through Psalm 23 and then John 10 and I think it was somewhere during the sermon about gatekeepers, shepherds, and teachers that I noticed a lesson, even though you could say it was just coincidence, on Mary Jo's head because the chemo had taken her hair and she had taken the wigs and the scarves and put them away (we had hugged and laughed before church when I asked if she had changed her name to Yul) and she had chosen to sit in that exact spot , four pews in front of me, her head tilted in concentration just so the sun was just enough so the chandeliers – part of the old church, part of where her father had come – were reflected on her scalp, though not in their full form but as nova stars starting at her napped horizon and rising in a path to the crown of her head, a sky that shown not blue but as if there was smoke or an odd haze which meant the stars were incredibly bright to be noticed at all and led in an arcing path to the reflected stained glass window on her temple where the depictions of host and spirit and radiance were gone but there was a hint, a sense, they were not because they were actually shining more brightly so the detail was lost in the light and it was in that moment, that moment when we were all still though blood rushed and hearts pounded and air ran through lungs, that I understood the fallacy of all the arguments of those who do not believe in anything because there on her head, *in her head*, was the message, the reality, that is the same for every one of us:

Each and every day, it is all just a matter of faith.

Gone Autumn

the world spins at war
yet, at this moment
deciduous revel in October bacchanal
and evergreen prepare to test strength
holding fallen clouds

the world spins at war
yet, at this moment
worship and adulation in a leaf
plucked from a maple
gone autumn

Gradients

Parallel poems

evenings, after the first frost
close to the second, the grass

                                        they lie together,
                                        motionless

winter's protection
held in a deeper green

                                        held in a deeper breath

there has been rain
though, the moon

                                        a breath rises, waves
                                        in open window light

edges of leaves,
surfaces of grass, split it

for Elizabeth McFarland and my friend, Daniel Hoffman

38

Hale-Bopp, April 1997

Delicate
lace
folded to wind
unseen

sky veil of frost
covering
time's landscape
and spring ground

He is blind and asked

He is blind and asked about the picture
in the wood grain of the door

Do you understand
know what grain is?

Yes. Rings.

How do I explain what cutting
along the length of the log does
that the rings are not circles
what happens when a plane, parallel
intersects, top to bottom,
parts of an irregular cylinder

Would the mathematics of topology
explain to his fingers:

what is focus
how staring intently
loses it and finds:

the Madonna on a pumpkin
the old man in the borders of New Jersey

a message or a wish

I think that's close to it:
a wish come through eyes
made almost blind

remembering David Simpson

40

How do you follow "tasting God"?
after a line by Michael Glaser

I laid down
in the dirt
in spring
on the morning after it had rained all night
leaving just crisp and bright

I laid down in this:
the dew - yes, there was dew
on top of the rain on top of the grass -
and it soaked through my clothes
layered my skin
and we warmed together

together we felt the earth
new again, though she was very old
awaking, though she had slept very long
and together - the dew, the earth and I -
we listened to a crocus
piercing from under to above
and together, we waited for her

she arrived
and we breathed
together the air and the sound
we smelled and heard
and we touched each other -
yes, we touched
each other

my lips to earth, grass and dew
to crocus and air

A hurricane goes through many stages as it develops. It starts, most often, as a tropical wave drifting off of the western coast of Africa; a moving area of low pressure, it feeds on the warm waters of the equatorial Atlantic, organizes and grows stronger.

Non-Hodgkin Lymphoma: any of a large group of cancers of the immune system, many not curable, marked by lymph nodes enlarged by concentrations of cancerous cells that spread via the lymph and blood systems.

Hurricanes
Of Katrina and a daughter's cancer

Preface: Remembering

4 AM
*a truce is signaled
in the shuddered catch
of a shared breath*

*my sleep is lost to the vision
of a four-month-old's fingernail*

About twenty-seven years later

Katrina, certainly larger than quantum
fluctuations that begin to spiral
drift westward off the coast of Africa
a gentle wave bathed in sunlight
it feeds

*maybe not larger than quantum
fluctuations that begin to spiral
drift along hidden pathways
a quiet anarchy bathed in a rich life
it feeds*

About a month later

Katrina
a tsunami in slow motion
deliberate and random
defined and circular
her warnings unheeded
a truth beyond telling and seeing

the wind is one of numbers
the constant speed of birth
the constant lack of dying
exponential in yield
and the peripheral strike out
colonize again

Five and half months later, Valentine's Day

Noon: off to find a bathroom
a moment to wander among new things
unbroken things without mold
after standing in everything broken
everything molded, everything there but gone
a stop sign commands to stand and look
even though you could not look enough
at a tree, twisted like a rope or cable split open
pulled together again though its strength is gone,
its roots firmly planted, still defiant but
about the height of one person up, the bend is graceful
the falling almost seems, possibly, gentle
as if placed to rest by fingers of wind
left there to die, roots firmly planted
still defiant

3 PM: there is not a shudder with the ring
nor even a breath caught moving in step with the breeze
but with the words heard there is a thrust, sudden and violent
beneath, then behind the sternum
then lifting and spinning
then the tossing of or against anything
and then the closing in

though arms of friends and strangers hold
try to stop the falling, it almost matters not
it is all the thought of her ... alone
of fate and the unknown

Seventy-two hours later

noting again wind
how turning perpendicular brings almost silence
but even with backing into it
you can not ignore
truth or metaphor:
pain and spirit
rocks and tears in eyes

and through contrived silence
hearts pounding
louder and alone

Postscript: Reminding

listening to this place
there is water:

crashing below cliffs
of an island I have not seen

in a lake so vast it curves
rising to meet heaven

there is water in this place
where rain has fallen
along oak leaves and maple
gutters and streams

in this full glass

in this breath that fogs

there is water here

in this place smaller
in veins and capillaries
pressing the walls of cells
deep within this place
where the smallest pieces bend
in a pattern as wings
they move as if they fly

there is water in this place
between where even space becomes as sand

this is where we stand
and there is water

listen

I am listening:

This is where we stand
and there is water

Listen

"I am" is listening

I sit in darkness, walk in light

"But by the grace of God, I am what I am"
I Corinthians 15:10

I sit in darkness, walk in light
I sit in darkness, walk in light

The Reverend Swanson pleads
Place no smiley face on the wound!
We must see the boil, taste the puss!
He is nearly crying, his book of hate held high
Please, please no smiley face on the wound!

I sit in darkness, walk in light

Because I let my children read magical books
I must drown them, he commands
millstones about their necks
to give them time to feel *my sin*
saving them from my sin, their own inevitable sin

I sit in darkness, walk in light

After the meeting, the little lesbian girl
enfolds me, whispers to me, *how can you*
love me when you don't even know me?
My mother doesn't love me!
crying, then through tears
How can you? I love you!

I sit in darkness, walk in light

I teach your children
I love them, too –
the girls who love girls
the boys who love boys
and the ones who hide in darkness –

Because I, too, sit in darkness
walk in light, yet cast no shadow
because that which is "I", sits in darkness

I sit in darkness, walk in light
I sit in darkness, walk in light

For Catherine

In light that will come

don't you wish you could hear
the conversations we see

as the moon, in first eighth
falling into the last edge of sunset,

must be happy: the hint of crow's feet
and dimples tightening from a smile

to be certain, there is something being said
just as during the quarters and the full

and as much as in the new:
when the dark is not all dark

because of conversations we hear and see
in light that comes from us

and in light that will come

In the rain you barely feel

in the rain you barely feel
it is the leaves you hear
not the grass bending under
the weight of water

it is the exponential of trees
the way they fall water

and then, too, the wind
bending and adding paths
or changing them
accelerating the louder

press the grass with your palm
as your dog lies gathering a stick
watch the sound work
and a flood begin

Innabah

how in May
the water that is wind
is captured by moss
that is new green and soft leaves
and the sound of the falls
       written high in the trees
becomes birdsong
and the clearing becomes a pond
nearly a mirror except for the gentle grass
and reflection is bright around

Confirmand retreat
May 6, 2006

Lagrange Point: one of five positions in an orbital configuration where a small object affected only by gravity can theoretically be stationary relative to two larger objects

Lagrange Point

far enough from both to balance

up the hill, away from the lake
and its reflections of autumn, sun,
moonlight and even clouds
its shoreline, islands and clarity
smooth stones and reeds
its effect on air

but not high enough
to be able to turn into the wind
on the ridgeline, to single out trucks
and cars on the Neck Road
to smell exhaust
but enough to feel more of the sun

far enough from both to balance

on a boulder more hidden in the earth than seen
to sit among birch and poplar, oak and maple
more young than old
some that had survived

in balance

isolated from all except
a commonality behind closed eyes:

how waves sound like wind
bring a forest close without a tree in sight

how wind through colors of autumn sounds
like waves rolling across sand and dwindling to foam

It must happen like this
A battlefield flashback

first, listen to April mid-night rain –

                    percussive

small hands on overturned plastic pails
            intermittently touching
resigned to different strengths
            none strong
                    barely weak

a few fingers finger the sides

occasionally, a firmer strike:
            a stick on a wood block

some small plastic pellets fall into a bucket
            almost filled

sand slides through an hour-glass figure
            with hips sheared away at the waist
            dropping onto copper sheets

these are just normal sounds of rain
they drain through gutters easily
            in small waves of drowning

it is an hour or two before the radared red storm arrives
            with its cracks and echoes
            with its strobe and instant shadow

there are crickets, hidden, chirping

there is a cat:
asleep on the man's chest
placing an outstretched paw
in his hand

              ... and then there is another sound

it comes unannounced from within

               ... and then there is a memory that is smell

and then ...

         ... and then ...

               ... and then ...

The art of "lectio divina" begins with cultivating the ability to listen deeply,
hear "with the ears of our hearts"
Fr. Luke Dysinger, O. S. B. from "Accepting the Embrace of God: The Ancient Art of
Lectio Divina"

Lectio

Selected Scripture – Mark 4: 33 – 41

Begin with the picture on the wall:

A blue-gray house
not dissimilar to the water it overlooks
darker than the sky that looks upon it
with different grasses in different response to breeze
in different response to season
as a shrub leafless appearing dead
though growing as if from it
colored as if the fusion of twigs and branches
an extension of grass climbing the home
on a chimney that parallels far on the horizon
the single white line of a sail

Begin *Lectio*, try to clear:

Centering, the first thought:
there is a woman who told these stories
this story, confidently, to all the children
they entrusted her with His word and their children

At sea, a storm arose; yet she found love
in arms they said were forbidden
those of another woman

They were afraid and fearful of their ship sinking
They abandoned her while reaching for their children
sought to save their boat by casting her into the sea

Scripture, two readings:

Mark recalls how
they put out onto that sea, to cross
as He said they should
a distance that must have been blue-gray
even in sunlight without a storm
though a storm did come
with wind that blew white-capped waves into their boats
while He slept and they cried of perishing
He woke rebuking the wind and sea, "Peace!
Be still!" Then, turning to them, "Why are you afraid?
Have you no faith?"

Mark said He always spoke in parables
But explained everything in private to His disciples

The third reading:

"He woke and rebuked the wind
And said to the sea 'Peace! Be still!'
The wind ceased and there was dead calm."

I wonder which are the parables
or when they become parables
wish to see direction in His simple words

the sea accepts them, life accepts them
in their boats, as they are

what holds them on their journey?

The answer is in His question

The fourth reading:

"Have you still no faith?"

at His word – peace
stillness, calm accepted all

We are all made in His image
we all are
in His image

Peace. Be still.
Have faith.

End with prayer:

I hold up my sister who found love
where You put it, where You led her

I hold her up now as a house become a home
though with fewer paths leading through grass to her door

I hold her overlooking a sea that may find a storm
though a sea calm in our sight

I hold my sister and her love listening to the voice across the water
a single sail set on our horizon

Peace. Be still.
Why are you afraid?
No storm will hurt you.

I hold you up, my sister
I hold you up

For Rachel

Less worried about the wind

My maple is dying
though painted in March against high clouds
add a full moon, she looks as alive
as the others bending
less worried about the wind

My maple is dying
though she is not really mine
we have been just acquaintances
she handing squirrels to my attic, holding chimes
lessening worry about the wind

My maple is dying
though she still has time
to cradle birds and babies next to my window
and so tease the cats on the sill
she still dances at this age
less worried about the wind

Light Rain

waiting
we could have curled
together anywhere you could have
focused on a flower discerning
color in the darkness by closing your eyes
my hand cupped next to your heart
your neck the same to me
        eyes closed or open
we could have waited longer
for the Perseid rain to weave
through our imagination
we could have waited for light to rain
but it already had

Painting the history of an old tree

if you must, you must
just please cut across below the knee
through the ankle would be best
there you can find the first ring

then, if the blade is fine
a little more time
a tad of sun, rain
movement of mercury

place your brushes
away with the oils, no need
for anything except fingers
and their hearing from touch

of the long low notes
from pulling across the rings
after the heart of each has inhaled
what air is left

pull from the center out
and there will be a song from the beginning:
first darkness, the moisture and warmth
the sun, moon, rain

long winters of snow, long years of drought
there will be wind, if you listen
carefully, drawing across the waves
of it, you will feel the dance

more easily than the stars:
the barely perceptible overtones, harmonies
from the moment she, a seed, fell one night
carried away to a soft fold in the earth

of my old, dying maple

Of Venus and First Lt. Dawn Halfaker
Alive Day June 19, 2004

"It all seems now to have been a dream." from "With Her" by Creslaw Milos

They say Venus, Aphrodite, would have been adorned
painted, jeweled, contemplating an apple in her left
hand raised, her right lowered, draped across
a drape on her knee, mysteriously held by her hips
or maybe mysterious isn't the word
while dreaming, thinking
Of what?

Dawn, modern flesh, was stoic as well, clothed,
seated, plain green sweater, not jeweled, jeans
the same gaze to hold you, unwavering
confident voice as, you would think
Aphrodite, Venus, commanding gently
though maybe here dreaming as she spoke
Of what?

Venus speaks in marble of goddess
this goddess speaks in flesh of war
and moment, when breathing stops
you, and her, together, in her night-
marish-like, ghostlike, you hear her
not speak, then whisper her real fear
Of what?

That starts with loving and being loved
if ever, of making love, if ever
of making life, if ever, of giving birth
if ever that would be so ... wonderful
to love together and cherish her child
together, though her fear, alone
Of what?

Of holding, of wanting to, of a child
needing her mother to
with two arms when she only has
one, her fear, what stops her
her fear
Of what?

Unable to feel her child
safe in her two arms

People with mental illness or cognitive development issues surround us; most of the time we chose not to notice them. When we are forced to notice, we often cross to the other side of the street, move away or ask that someone else move them out of sight. By not noticing, we ignore a part of ourselves, shun brothers or sisters, fail to admit how they are is not their fault and how easily it could have been us. By turning aside and walking away we learn and teach how not to love.

Monuments

streams that start in the middle of a field
and other things that are not supposed to be

after decades I finally started to see them
as monuments, before they had been incongruities

I found one monument
in a high field, though I needed a guide
to show me the gash hidden
falling down from the mountain
a shadow you almost couldn't see

difficult to understand the beginning
it could have been going up as easily as down
a war of boulders flung
trees and plants ripped by weather
relentless: a way to take away

it is not as simple as walking
from the meadow to the edge of the arroyo
though there were trees to show you
how they have grown
differently: gnarled but still graceful

far below there is a stream
a trickle in the darkness
it shines in reflected gaze
of those who find and understand:

the sun sets westerly, at the right time
through the nearly leafless tree, the sculptor adds
the flame again, alive to your touch, the hands reach
(as his, smooth and slender, delicate even in the end)
they move in whispers following the wind

For Nick and all the others

Notes on a translator's notes

*... in the seven-hundred-year-old city of Sanok in southeastern Poland. The wall
of his patio adjoins a Franciscan church, where his **ancestors are buried (1)**,
the church also serves as a **repository for their birth (2)**, baptism and
death certificates (3). This **proximity to the ancestral (4)** crypt is a
constant reminder of his forebears' absence and presence ... ***

(1) ancestors are buried

that which is *I*
comes mostly from before, the *not I*:

ancestors are buried
everywhere and nowhere, throughout

and if without reproduction
then certainly when they crawled or walked
ran or just fell in dying, returning

so the part that was them
and the part that was *not-them*
> became parts again

(2) repository for their birth

each in its own way is a vault
that each breaks into, opens
steals the delicate tables
onto which life, a new *I*, is placed

(3) death certificates

prove life

(4) proximity to the ancestral

I am thinking

I am listening

64

occasionally I will hear
or I will think I hear

and occasionally I will feel
or I will think I feel

but, mostly, it is all of that
as much as none of that

it is, however, a door
I and *not-I* lean on, always

* *"Translator's Note" by Ewa Hryniewicz-Yarbough on "Klara" by Janusz Szuber*
"Poetry", April 2007; Volume CXC, Number 1; pages 12 – 13

Pascagoula ghosts

Long after Katrina, the residents
have gone back to their repaired homes
the abandoned temporary trailer parks
are marked only by white sewer pipes
and a streetlamp or two

skeletons
without heads
just spines and ribs

bake
in southern gulf sun
above high-water marks

glow
oddly
at night

while cats stalk
there is quiet
now

the ghosts
moved
barely turn a head

when passing, remembering
because skeletons without heads
are their bones

are what they still feel

Process

it started with driving
driving past the stream
the stream I drive by everyday
this day it was noon
this day it was winter
the scene of photographs
the topic of poems, setting of stories

it started with noticing form
remembering the form of summer or fall
a rope laid on an uneven floor
the form of the lowest points tied
tied through fallen trees
around rocks, around larger curves
larger curves which were in spring larger
which means straightened by water overflowing

it all started by noticing form
the form of now, the form of winter
winter and ice leaving only the deepest channel
leaving only the heart of life
the flow of life
life not smooth but ragged
ragged with edges and sharp turnings
turnings from crashes
crashes that move you

it started by noticing

First, look.

Second, many paths can lead to the same place; all are valid but just because a path appears obvious does not mean that it is.

Third, touch.

Place

First

an inch of fresh snow
rabbit tracks
four paws together
forward and returning
in either dark still night
or the silence of dawn
the echo of hesitations
between leaps, glances
a signature

Second

I fell between two places of certainty

as with Newton's iteration
even with the solutions known
there is chaos in the boundaries, in the whole
unexpected pathways to that certain certainty *

as there is with the reading of
"I am the way"
is that the only ... *way*
or an example of many
as the Greek may imply

there must be many
as there are many of us
and *way* is often just an other
that falls to a certain certainty
unexpectedly falls to thought

falls to the way whole

Third

unexpected perfection
in a single rose
petals : lips :
parting, drawing invitation
nearly drowned in noon's height, drinking
shadows lengthen and
warmth : light captured :
escapes slowly

the rose speaks

     touch

* *"Chaos" by James Gleick (1987, Penguin Books)*
  Color plate "The Complex Boundaries of Newton's Method"
  After page 114

Schuylkill

been told it means *hidden river*
though, personally, the Dutch is unknown
unfortunate it is not known

                being *schuyl*
on this hillside, so as to find
deer, stand downwind beside
and hawks, though they would sense

                what is *quiet*
in Dutch on this hillside to sit
with this river, deer, and hawk
and leaves from an autumn almost done

                what is *sunset*
here on the hillside then on the *kill*
the *schuyl* one holds the hills
the last pieces of season and sun

                almost *schuyl*
the *kill* sliding silently
brushing underneath a turning sky
black with brown birds seeking shore

                I am *schuyl*
on this hillside, imagining
I am *kill* slipping silent
imagining I see

Seeking silence

is difficult. And I'm speaking of the exercise,
the search, the effort and work in the task
in the wake of a death or losing your job and here
it was both, too close together. The voices came:
from outside, from within and there isn't a moment's
peace because of the questions and silence becomes
an abstraction, something more, if you will, than
the relative it already was, And while it was me
that changed, not silence, I reasoned it was a matter
of listening well, of watching more closely for it to jump out:

in a moment ...

Jane's eyelids began to fall, caught, fell on top of each other
as if landslides from the news on mute, inexorable if you want
inescapable on foot as was the echo that rang at the same time
the padding of her cat across the floor though the cat had died
and the fire in the stove was following, the steam in the pot
quieting so that let the rain, and the little ice, chat on the sill
and the African violet pant in mid-labor birthing a new lavender
while the streetlamp's light chorused into more than altos, tenors
and sopranos while passing through the glass which
itself had begun to settle into its own night, thinking of its age

seeking silence.

Shadow

the definition of love
beyond time, gender and sameness

reminds of felt
and in melancholy
the closeness of another hand is memory

but, also with the sun
that warmth will come again
if indeed it ever left

for Daniel Hoffman

The advent of angels

It was not a leap, just a calculation I hoped would work when I asked the students, "Who in this room has cancer?" Not expecting any hands to rise, one did, and I noticed, shocked, but moved on to "Who in this room has someone in their family – parent, brother, sister, aunt, uncle or cousin – who has cancer?" and five out of ten hands rose. It was a calculation to lead to a conversation about why we do all these things in school so that when you are a father or a mother and your daughter makes you one of those five hands you know how to learn, investigate, write, ask, decide, to stand beside. After class, that one hand that rose in answer to my first question stood beside me: clutching her books to her chest, pretty, long dark brown high school hair – straight, shimmering, luscious, reaching the small of her back. "Leukemia" and "Three years ago" and "Cured" is what I heard as she told me her story while I thought of her bald or left with just wisps of hair while on a bed with tubes in her arms. She was trying not to cry as she said, "Your daughter will be fine. I know she will. *I. Know. She. Will.* Don't worry, everything will be okay." She left. I was speechless, frozen, and convinced. You are never prepared for this – the advent of angels.

Of Marcella

73

Something happened first

Genesis 1:14 – 19
Mike, detonated October 1952, yield – 10.4 MT
Continental Flight 177, November 15, 2004

Something happened first
and what happened began
the first day

Something happened first
and what happened created
light on the first day

Something happened first
their need that bore the idea
to re-create what happened on the fourth day

Something happened first
acceptance, then creation of what would bear
bomb light on the chosen day

Something happened first
and they wanted to capture it but knew
they could only watch from afar as it passed

Something happened first
that caused the Army captain to be on the plane
with us from Philadelphia to Houston

Something happened first
and they asked us to wait
so the Army captain could leave before us

Something happened first
that required the Army captain to be there
at attention when the cargo door first opened

Something happened first
that caused light to be locked in a box
shining, but not shining, at the end of a journey home

Something happened first
that caused words and light

Something happened first
that led to bombs that made light

Something happened first
that filled this box that reflected light

Something happened first
and they kept a picture now that it had passed

Some (inconsequential) truths about Key West

the horizon curves in all directions

...

in sun-white
the wave nature of light
captures a pelican:
the sine form of wings
traced over by the interference
of water with breeze

...

in the absence of moon-white
in the absence of sight or seeing
there is little hearing
in the welcoming of
Thomas Victor O'Toole
home

...

was there joy sometimes
praise or hope
in his story
was there thankfulness
from us

...

we stand at the top
everything curving in all directions
in sun-white, in moon-white
in the wave nature of light
speaking only sometimes
of praise and hope

Thomas Victor O'Toole
Veteran, homeless
Died January 9, 2008, Key West, Fl

Suicide by police

because I am not
a novelist, I
cannot use pages
to describe his anxiety
lonesome and lost, pacing
for hours within the stone mansion

nor a journalist, I
cannot use columns continued
on an interior page with art
capturing a dozen squad cars parked at angles
cops behind trees with weapons drawn
and snipers in camo prone

observing, I can
write of the darkness without moon
and the odd quiet in the neighborhood that night
the strange lack of press given the response
how we began in light jackets
and ended in parkas

as a neighbor, I
must admit I did not know him
nor his aunt or uncle or how he came to be there
why, on a night when we celebrated another's long life
he wanted to take his own, more than fifty years less
why he no longer cared to try

as a parent, I
tried to imagine the loss
remembered an admission I'd heard
stopped breathing once, thinking:
if I could not touch her hand
pull her back, feel her ...

as a poet, I
struggled for words of pain,
being lost and helpless
without contact in the world,
a world that does not reach out,
the reason that drives one to end

standing by, I heard
someone mumble, *Oh, for chrissake
it's Christmas week, I don't need this!*

this
I, human
do need, want, reach
feel helpless and silenced
weep when I hear six shots
mourn when I hear of his death

Christmas week, 2007

The anniversary of today

poems suggest

and while my brothers are not dead as hers,
my brother-in-law is, nine thousand days

today, an anniversary of sorts:

for one brother it was one more day
at work, at soccer matches with his son

for another with his wife
it was one more drive to The Cape

for my sister it was nine thousand eight hundred and fifty
days since she changed her name

and maybe thirty-six hundred days since she moved
to the little blue house though I'm not sure

for me it was almost nineteen thousand seven hundred and ten days
since my first and twenty-two since my job went away

I'm not sure how many days since the first daylily bloomed
or that I noticed two pairs of cardinals instead of just one

maybe next year I should write these down

it has been one hundred and fifteen days since cancer arrived
eleven since confirmation of remission

only twenty minutes since the little cat purred
curled up in the basket on my desk for a nap
and I'm wondering if that counts for anything
as she wraps her paw around my finger

forty-four days until one thousand eight hundred and twenty-six
officially together but two thousand five hundred and forty-seven
since her love arrived

I'll put off cutting the grass for a day
to celebrate the anniversary of yesterday
and a sunny afternoon

but tomorrow, I'm not sure what I'll do
to celebrate the anniversary of today

sca • lar [skey-ler] *adjective*: 1. Representable by position on a scale or line; having only magnitude.
noun: 1. A quantity possessing only magnitude.

The scalar nature of snow

elusive
if not rare

there are always vectors
and other values

if not measured
at least felt or experienced

at the boundary of ground
imbalance and, therefore, movement

the creation comes, then
with the condition of height and time:

eight stories up
suspended in a moment

binary values
of ones and zeroes –

just snow
or not snow –

no vectors of momentum
or spin

no description of unique shape
or crystalline order

just points to move between
floating to observe

as picking through pond lilies
or stars in the winter sky

there or not there
in this moment

the scalar nature of snow

The test

was a simple test to confirm
what we knew he did not know

one question was *Which is a part of your body:*
        A – hat; B – hand; C – sock?

His answer was *a sock.*

Writing his answers, the motion was elegance
        grace in the gradual
        suspense in the inevitable
as his head, as all of him, slipped
        closer to the table
as I waited for the pencil to stop
precisely filling in the circle marking his answer
        now with a line attached
        a string tied to a balloon
           rising to a cloud
        a tether remembering shapes
           it once touched

it was as if there was singing
        though it was not a tune or dissonance
it was readable in that it was watchable
especially with closed
        or closing
           eyes
noting the comfort of familiar

        lullabies

still, he fought the sleep
though with each drift away I asked
        did he dream when he went?

were they different from the ones he told me
each day before he took the dollar bill I offered
        hid it in his hand for a moment
        then folded it into
                his sock

These ghosts

this ghost in my house heard
the sprinkler across the street at midnight
came, sat down next to me, and asked
Rain?
no, it hadn't rained, wasn't raining
No, rain.
and there was a certainty
somehow, it had been rain

this ghost in my house is black
which is unique as they are always
white as was she
beautiful fog in a night without moon or stars
and still, she smiles *It is a trick of shadows and light*
not desire to be white

this ghost in my house is a new one
he held out his hand
said it had been nearly orange before
the way the moon is sometimes
he remembered how his eyes had been
yellow moons that kept trying to rise
that kept falling back below their horizons
now he turned his hand, marveling at his fingers
So simple is what he said

this ghost in my house just stares
and though silent, she makes no surprise
she looks, then turns
then looks again
it's her eyes:

see with her eyes in the night
day birds are sleeping
seek an owl
and the soft pressing of air

Valley Forge Park well after sunset: Deer

there is a sense of motion / not movement as much as the change in air
from heat so, even the sense is an illusion drawn / from an inability to
perceive through the stillness / search, anticipate, and wait

the headlight that will soon blind / begins its turn through this space and
the earliest incident shines / across grass tops that soften and hide

sparks of diamond blue haze / rise from deep within un-protected humour
there is no turning / except for the light

then there is a sense of motion / locked in the retina from burning
in waves as if the air moves from heat / and though there is stillness

a sense

(location – hillside across from parking lot on Rt. 23 near the covered bridge)

Ms. Dana Hirsch is a resident of Inglis House, a full-time care facility for clients with severe physical disabilities. She is also an excellent poet. Ms. Marilyn Monroe is an icon, a standard of beauty, and in her last days, quite possibly, isolated and alone. These two women, in many respects, are worlds apart but in the parts that bring us together as human they may be the same.

One difference, however, is that Ms. Monroe has a wine named after her and each annual vintage's bottle is adorned with a different picture from her life. I have several on a bookshelf overlooking my desk. On one, leaning forward temptingly in a white strapless dress, almost out of the label, her eyes seem to tell a different story.

Ms. Hirsch may be found in several pictures documenting the Inglis House Poetry Conference
.

Two women

neither I know
though I drink both

one stares at me
over me, beyond me
through me from a bottle of wine
lilting forward, offering
a guide to stare somewhere
common, but pleading
if we but knew

one stares at me
from a wheeled chair
at me, through me
at ... me
lilting backward
reaction to action
laughing to guide
a stare somewhere
uncommon, pleading
if we but knew

the story of rain
of conversations with windows
and the cries
alone

for Dana Hirsch and Marilyn Monroe

What do you make

what do you make
   of a single red tulip
      the only bloom
         in a garden

do you make desolation
   and the last of things
      a failed life
         where nothing will grow

what do you make
   if you stop, see
      the irises beginning
         the pachysandra greening

notice even the chickweed
   parting for the wild violets
      the pear blossoms raining
         from any spring sky

what do you make
   of a single red tulip

When one is lost

"Without a witness, they just disappear." – from "Taking Chance"

how are these mountains diminished
or these wheat fields bending
these lakes and streams

how are these cities less
or these states
these counties and towns

how is the ocean changed
or this night
these planets, stars, even space

how are all these different
when *any one* is lost
too soon to war

What if Eve

What if Eve
had just been listening, intent
in conversation with the stream about water
of life with the earth, about giving birth
what if she was just speaking
to women about women

What if Eve
never actually bothered with the serpent
other than a nod of good afternoon
because she saw through his insincere hissing
dismissing him, understanding
his character as women do

What if Eve
had learned on her own the joy
in the blue sameness of a robin's egg and the sky
in digging her toes into earth's soft skin
in playing finger games with the stream
what if she did this without an apple

What if it was Adam
just a young curious boy
just as all young boys since
reckless and fearless
and lying when caught
blaming the girl

What if God saw all this
gave Adam, gave men
the opportunity to change, accept
their mistake but they did not
and they blustered their lie more loudly
covering their guilt with the serpent's knowledge

What if God touched Eve
an instant later for Him, millennia for us
gave her the gift of true knowledge
told her to rise and use it
told her to save His creation

What if Eve stands, listens, then speaks

for Corinne

While contemplating beauty

we are built upon uncertainty
that which we will never see

we are just energy
no more different from light
than from a flower

and thought: a perception
a gift, though yet we choose
more often fear

something apart
rather than us
light or a flower

Wisteria

of Susan

there was some speculation
about her beginning
whether a bird had dropped a seed
in the normal fashion, in the way of plants
or had someone sown specifically

but, how ever it had been
she took him, the pine, to be her own
a spindly runner whose gait had been lost
whose arms flailed at air formlessly

together they had become sky

                              dusk
on those certain nights, lavender
color and fragrance mixed
it seemed there was a breeze
                              but gentle
and clouds not quite distinct
and at the edge   honeysuckle

William Carlos Williams, the first time
O'Hare Airport, Terminal 3, Concourse G, Gate 19, 7:30 AM

I like to think
I notice more than most
until I realize I've missed so much
when I read, I understand that
when I walk or drive or run
        or fly or breathe
I understand that

This morning, reading William Carlos Williams for the first time
the "Pastoral" about the old man gathering dog-lime
and his majestic tread, was that him I saw in her?

Just then, her broom rattled to the floor and before she could bend
to pick it up. three men, fully young enough to be her grandchildren
or even great-grand, stepped over it without a notice

I noticed, but from too far away

After they had swept up the hall in youthful, excited gait,
she gathered her broom back, continued on her way,
her job was the trashcans, her route down this side,
around the end and back and there blossomed
the questions in so many forms:

Why was she here? Who was she elsewhere?
What could I discern of all that?

She took the look of a grandmother (maybe my grandmother
who had died twenty years before), the broad collar of her blouse,
embroidered white on white, as if it were lace, hung outside her smock,
her silver hair neat and curled, she wore matte red lipstick
and soft makeup.

A gentle smile joined her face.

Her gait was slow, methodical, there was a new trashcan
every twenty feet or so, down to the end, around and back,
she touched each one, wiped it clean as if they were her own.

There was no phone at her hip or ear, no music that I could hear,
as if, I imagined, she was listening at home, alone, curtains and lamp
shades fringed and drawn, rugs from a time when her collar would have
been lace, not far from here, I think, her place.

Maybe I'm wrong but to borrow the poet's memorable line:

These things astonish me beyond words *

*from "Pastoral" by William Carlos Williams

Acknowledgements

Big Bridge - "A prayer drawn from Holy War"
Forward (Fox Chase Cancer Center) - "The advent of angels"
God and Nature ~ "Entropy and Enthalpy"
Mad Poets Journal - "62998", "A breath", "A thought in the wake",
"Clear in New Hampshire", "Contemplating a life"
Scientific American - "The scalar nature of snow"

In my poem, "Notes on a translator's notes," I quoted from
"Translator's Note" by Ewa Hryniewicz-Yarbough on the poem, "Klara,"
by Janusz Szuber, Poetry, April 2007; Volume CXC, Number 1; pages 12-
13 (Poetry Foundation, Chicago, IL)

In my poem, "Bob," I quoted from "The Name" by Tomas Transtormer,
translated by Robert Bly, as it appears in "A New Path to the Waterfall"
by Raymond Carver, 1989, page 17 (The Atlantic Monthly Press, New
York, NY)

www.ingramcontent.com/pod-product-compliance
Lightning Source LLC
Chambersburg PA
CBHW030848090426
42737CB00009B/1154